A Book about HOMESCHOOLING

Allison's Story

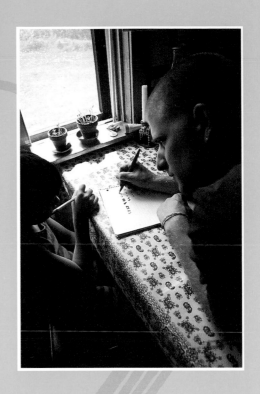

Jon Lurie
Photographs by Rebecca Dallinger

Ŀ LERNER PUBLICATIONS COMPANY / MINNEAPOLIS

*For Allison and the courageous
homeschool families of America.*

Illustrations by John Erste.

LIBRARY OF CONGRESS CATALOGING-IN-PUBLICATION DATA

Lurie, Jon.
    Allison's story : a book about homeschooling / Jon Lurie ;
photographs by Rebecca Dallinger.
        p. cm. — (Meeting the challenge)
    Summary: Describes the experiences of an eight-year-old girl and her
family who are educating their children at home.
    ISBN 0-8225-2579-8 (alk. paper)
    1. Home schooling—United States—Juvenile literature. [1. Home
schooling.] I. Dallinger, Rebecca, ill. II. Title. III. Series.
LC40.L87 1996
649'.68—dc20   95-49735

Manufactured in the United States of America
1 2 3 4 5 6 JR 01 00 99 98 97 96

Contents

MY NAME IS ALLISON, and I'm eight years old. I'm in third grade. But I don't go away to school each morning, like many of my friends do. I am schooled at home. That's what "homeschooling" means. My teachers are my mom and dad. My little sisters are my classmates. Gemma is five. She's in kindergarten. Martha is two. She's in preschool.

At eight o'clock in the morning, I'm the first person awake in my family. I don't have an alarm clock. My eyes open when it's time to get up. Morning is my favorite time. It's nice and quiet when my sisters and parents are asleep and I get to be alone. I brush my teeth and wash my face, then I go outside to feel the weather. It's a warm day, so I'll wear shorts.

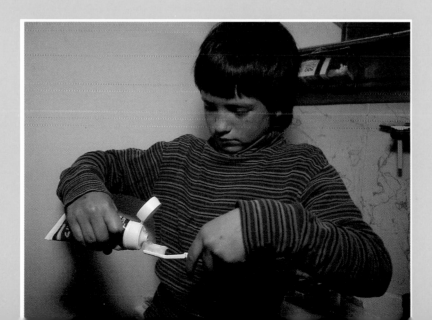

For breakfast, I make cereal with milk. I know how to cook lots of things. I can make eggs, fruit salad, regular salad, toast, and ants on a log. To make ants on a log, you spread peanut butter on celery and put raisins on top. It's yummy.

Mom and Dad expect me to make my bed, get dressed, wash, have breakfast, and get started on my schoolwork by nine o'clock. They stay up very late at night doing their work. Mom left me a note on the table with my morning assignments. She does this every day. I'm supposed to start my schoolwork right after breakfast.

But I don't feel like doing my lessons yet. I'd rather read. My favorite part of homeschool is when I get to read. My parents started teaching me to read when I was four. I can still remember the first word I learned. It was "Fan," the name of the cow in a story. The longest book I've ever read was 10 chapters. The book was called *27 Cats Next Door*. My favorite cat in the story was old and gray.

I find a good book to read. We have about 500 children's books in our house. I've read many of them, but there's always something new. I listen to Bach or Vivaldi's *Four Seasons* on the tape player while I read.

After a couple of chapters, I go to the kitchen table to do my work. The kitchen is also my classroom. My morning work is hard—math and spelling. Most of my lessons are about things that I choose to study. But every morning I have to do lessons that I wouldn't choose.

From nine o'clock until ten, I study spelling. I carefully write out the words on the list Mom left for me. I spell each word five times in my spelling notebook. Writing a word many times helps me remember how to spell it. I use a chart with all the letters on it to help me write each letter as neatly as I can.

My parents get up at ten o'clock. Dad starts teaching as soon as he gets out of bed. He makes lessons out of everything. This morning, he pretends we're in a restaurant. He tells me to take the family's orders for breakfast. Mom wants coffee and two pancakes. Gemma orders pancakes, yogurt, pizza, and french fries. Martha asks for Gummi Bears, popcorn, food, and juice. I give the orders to Dad. He makes pancakes for all of us. Martha cries for Gummi Bears. Dad tells me what everything at his restaurant costs. He asks me to add up everyone's bills and collect their money.

Let's see. Mom's two pancakes cost 50¢ each. Her coffee costs 35¢. So her bill comes to $1.35. She gives me $2.00 and tells me to keep the change. That means I have to subtract $1.35 from the $2.00 she paid. I give my Dad $1.35 for Mom's meal. I keep 65¢ for myself. Lessons that are part of real life are the kind I like best. They aren't like work—they're fun.

AFTER WE EAT, Dad checks my math and spelling from the breakfast orders I wrote down. I got two wrong on my math. We figure out why I got the problems wrong, and I try again. Sometimes I forget to carry my numbers. I rework the problems until I get them right.

The words I misspelled on the breakfast orders are added to my vocabulary list. There are five words to add: bear, dollar, orange, pancake, and juice. From ten-thirty until eleven o'clock, I carefully write the new words in my notebook. I have to concentrate to remember how each word is spelled. Mom gives me a spelling test once a week. She will give me one tomorrow.

At eleven o'clock, I work on multiplication tables. On nice days like this, I get to do my lessons outside. My dad and I make flash cards out of a cardboard box. I use them to quiz myself. I used to have trouble remembering the answers. But now I know my 1s, 2s, 3s, 4s, 5s, 6s, 10s, and 11s really well. I learn multiplication by studying just 10 problems at a time. I'm focusing on the 7s. After lunch I have to take a quiz on my 7s. Dad quizzes me often. He wants to see how well I remember what I've learned.

After half an hour, I get tired of studying flash cards. So I play a math board game that Mom and I made. My mom made the board. I drew all the artwork for it myself. To win the game you have to get through a haunted forest, go over a troll bridge, watch out for quicksand, and enter the magical multiplication palace. If you get the wrong answer, you might be eaten by a dragon or get lost in the evil bat cave.

Next, I practice typing on the computer. We have special programs just for kids. After a few minutes, I complete level three. Mom switches the program to a harder level. It's hard not to look at the keyboard while I type, but I'm getting better all the time.

My sister Gemma wants to use the computer, too. She always wants to do what I'm doing. I like to teach her things I've learned. Doing that helps me remember what I know. I teach her so much that I bet she'll be even smarter than I am someday. But she's driving me crazy and won't leave me alone. I get really mad and I cry.

I get tired of being with my whole family all the time. I like to go on special outings alone with just Mom or Dad. We all need to get away once in a while.

At twelve-thirty, Mom says it's recess time. I close my books and run outside. I have an hour to ride my bike, play in my fort, and play at the park with my sisters.

AFTER RECESS, Dad helps me read our weather station. We keep a chart of the temperature, wind, rainfall, and clouds. We've been waiting to plant our broccoli seedlings until the weather is just right. Mom gave me a gardening book last week. I read in the book that gardeners should plant seedlings in the spring after the last frost. This is the 10th day of warm weather in a row. Mom helps us find a perfect spot. Gemma, Martha, and I plant our seedlings in the garden.

For lunch, Mom serves my sisters and me a picnic. She cuts the sandwiches like butterflies, just the way we like them. When I'm a mom, I'll make picnics for my kids during homeschool.

At two o'clock, it's time for my science lesson. Today we're taking a field trip to the woods near our house. We get to see what we discover. I find some little black creatures swimming in the ditch. We carefully scoop them out of the puddle. We take them back to a water hole by our house.

Mom says they're tadpoles. She teaches us about amphibians (am-FIHB-ee-uhns) from a book called *Keepers of the Earth.* Amphibians are animals. Most amphibians spend the first part of their lives in water and the second part on land. The tadpoles will be frogs in the second part of their lives.

We'll learn more about the changes amphibians go through by watching the tadpoles grow. Gemma and I will keep track of the tadpoles' growth every day. We'll let them go free when they become frogs!

Mom teaches me the importance of amphibians to the earth. Amphibians are very fragile, she says. When an environment an amphibian lives in gets poisoned, amphibians are the first to die. I like knowing that I live in a healthy place.

Mom has me spell the words polliwog, tadpole, frog, and amphibian on the marker board. She tells me to add them to my word list.

At three-thirty, Dad says I have 10 minutes to study before the math quiz. My sisters get to go outside and play while I stay inside to study. It makes me mad when I have to work while they get to have fun.

"The quicker you do your work, the quicker you'll get to play," my Dad says.

I know he's right, but I wish I didn't have to take a test now.

Dad looks over my test. I hope I got them all right.

One wrong. Oh, 7 times 9 isn't 62?

Dad says the right answer is in my brain somewhere.

Oh yeah, 7 times 9 is 63. Right! I get to go out and play!

I play tag, hide-and-seek, and games my sisters and I make up. Then I do artwork. I draw, paint, weave, or make sculptures and crafts. I get my ideas from things I see, or things that my parents teach me. Other times I get ideas from books. This afternoon I'm making a construction paper Dimetrodon reptile.

WE HOMESCHOOL EVERY DAY. My cousin says homeschool isn't good because you don't get summers and weekends off. But homeschool doesn't mean I'm always sitting inside, doing work on paper. I learn from everything I do—even from paddling a kayak or building a tree fort. Some days I don't have to do any schoolwork. Other days, I spend seven or eight hours doing lessons. Sometimes my parents let me spend all day working on a special art or science project.

When I grow up, I want to be a potter, an artist, and a veterinarian. I love horses so much. Once in a while, my parents take me to a riding stable. I learn how to ride and take care of horses.

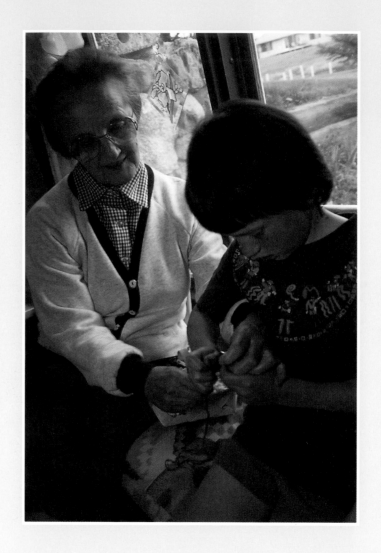

There are times when my parents can't teach me what I want to learn. Sometimes we read books and learn the answers together. Other times, my parents find someone else to teach me. Last week I asked Mom to teach me to knit. Grandma Mary, who lives across the street, taught me how. (She isn't really my grandma. My sisters and I call her that because she is like a grandma to us.) I knitted a tiny shirt for my doll so she can be warm at night when she kicks off the covers.

I also take dance lessons at a studio and art lessons at the muscum in the city. I want to learn about the whole world. Dad says that someday I'll be better at math than he is. Then his friend Greeny, a math teacher, will teach me. I want to go to college when I get older.

I don't always feel like doing my lessons. Homeschool isn't fun when I don't want to work. Then my parents get mad at me. They make me sit alone. I don't like sitting alone, but it helps me think. When I finally get my work done, I feel happy—very happy. My parents are happy, too, and proud of me. I get reward stickers and hugs when I try hard and do my work well.

MOST OF MY FRIENDS go to school. When we moved to a new town, I wanted to go to school so I could meet some kids. But then I became friends with a neighbor kid. I've made lots of new friends in the neighborhood.

Sometimes my parents have to drive me to see my friends. Most of them live too far for me to go alone.

Tonight we are going to have dinner with our friends at their house across the lake. Our friends live in a small village that you can only get to by boat. I've been looking forward to seeing my friends Lana, Lynn, and Richard the whole day.

We change into nice clothes for our visit. Dad helps us into our life jackets. We wait on our dock for Bryan, our friends' dad, to come for us. At half past six, he arrives.

I love seeing birds on the lake. There are some pelicans eating near shore tonight. Last week for homeschool I wrote a report on the pelicans we saw back in the marsh. My favorite part of the ride is going fast. I like it when it's windy and we go bump, bump, bump, on the big waves.

At our friends' house, I get to be silly and play and eat until my parents say it's time to go. I want to stay all night with my friends. But we have to leave before the sun goes down so Bryan can find his way back home. We say good-bye and snuggle together on the way home. It's cold on the lake at night.

Gemma and I put on our pajamas. Mom helps Martha with hers. Dad promises to read to us after 15 minutes of quiet time. I read from *Bunnicula*. It's a story about a rabbit who's also a vampire. All he does is suck the juice from carrots. I have to write three book reports before the end of the month. One of them will be on *Bunnicula*. Gemma tries to sound out words from one of her easy-reader books. Mostly she just looks at the pictures.

Mom calls me. She wants me to choose from a few books she has circled in a homeschool catalog. I really want a book about opera and a science kit. But the science kit isn't circled. Mom says if I choose the opera book, I can still get another book that will help me with spelling.

She and Dad agree to try to get me the science kit for my birthday. I wish we could do more science at homeschool. Science is fun. I want a real microscope and a chemistry set. We have to buy all of our classroom materials. We can't always afford to get everything we want.

It's ten-thirty. I'm sleepy. Dad reads us two stories from a Dr. Seuss book. Then he tells us a scary story. We love scary stories. I fall asleep wondering what I'll do tomorrow. I never really know what will happen because each day at homeschool is different. Maybe I'll have a history or geography lesson or put on a play with the whole family.

Mom comes over and says, "Hanble waste (hahn-BLAY wash-DAY)." That means "good dream" in the Lakota language. Lakota people once lived where we live now. "Hanble waste, Mom and Dad," Gemma and I say.

Mom and Dad sit together at the kitchen table while my sisters and I sleep. They discuss what we did and make plans for tomorrow. Mom went to school for six years to become a teacher. She has a master's degree in education. She's really, really smart.

Mom makes up the curriculum (kur-RIHK-yuh-luhm), or lessons, for our homeschool. Dad, Mom, and I set goals at the start of the school year. One of my goals is to learn all the multiplication tables by heart. When I've reached all my goals, I'll become a fourth grader!

Mom files my completed work and makes up tomorrow's lessons. Dad fills out a progress report in his homeschool journal. His homeschool journal is like a grade book. He keeps track of every lesson I do. These records will be my grades when I want to go to college.

Tomorrow, when I wake up, it'll be time to start another school day with my morning assignments. I think I'll stay in bed an extra hour and read. I can't wait to find out what happens to *Bunnicula*.

Information about HOMESCHOOLING

Before 1852, children in the United States were not required to attend school. That year, the state of Massachusetts passed a law that all children must go to a school approved by the government. Previously, some states had public schools or laws that required parents to teach their children at home. Soon every state in the union had laws regarding school attendance.

Because the United States Constitution does not address the question of education, each state is free to make its own rules. There are school attendance laws in all 50 states. Most states allow children to fulfill school attendance requirements by studying at home.

States that allow for homeschooling usually set guidelines for parents to follow so that children are well taught. States often set rules about aspects of homeschooling that affect students:

- the qualifications of the home instructor
- the language to be used during instruction (English or otherwise)

- the classes to be taught
- the amount of time that should be spent in instruction each day
- the number of days the child must be taught during the year
- the standardized testing schedule the child must take to determine progress
- the reports parents must submit to school officials

Parents choose to homeschool their children for many reasons. People who travel a lot, such as athletes, performing artists, and migrant farm workers, have long homeschooled their children by necessity. Families living in extremely remote areas often have no public school available. They may have no choice but to teach on their own. Some parents teach at home to uphold a religious tradition, while others keep their kids out of public school because they object to the political or cultural values being taught there. Gifted children or children having trouble adapting to the school environment are sometimes homeschooled to receive the extra attention they might need to succeed.

Many homeschool parents say they enjoy teaching and are happy to be able to spend more time with their children. If they are poor, homeschool can be a way to provide their children with an education they couldn't otherwise afford.

Certain benefits of homeschooling are often cited by homeschool parents. Many believe children learn best when they can set the pace of their lessons. Home teaching can be geared to each child's speed. Homeschool parents have the freedom to experiment with different teaching methods—to use those that work, and discard those that don't.

Homeschooling also has some drawbacks. Parents must devote a huge amount of time to their children's education. That leaves little time for earning money. In most homeschooling situations, the parents are required to provide all materials for teaching. Homeschool offers no organized extracurricular activities, such as sports or theater, which schools normally provide. Homeschoolers often have limited access to computers, films, and other resources found in most schools. Homeschooled children may miss spending the day with friends. Homeschool families who are not involved with other homeschoolers sometimes feel a sense of isolation, or being apart, from the general community.

Each homeschool is as unique as the parents and children who teach and learn in it. The pros and cons of homeschooling have been hotly debated since the days when the children of Massachusetts were first required to attend public school. Homeschools have many success stories. Other times, homeschool parents decide that their children would be better off in school.

Recent studies show a huge increase in the popularity of homeschooling. Estimates of the number of homeschooled children in the United States range from about 500,000 to one million, compared to the early 1980s, when only about 20,000 to 40,000 children were educated at home.

For Further READING

Colfax, David and Micki. *Homeschooling for Excellence*. Philo, Calif.: Mountain House Press, 1987.

Guterson, David. *Family Matters*. New York: Harcourt Brace Jovanovich, 1992.

Holt, John Caldwell. *How Children Fail*. New York: Delta/Seymour Lawrence, 1982.

Holt, John Caldwell. *How Children Learn*. New York: Delta/Seymour Lawrence, 1989.

Reed, Donn. *The Home School Source Book*. Bridgewater, Maine: Brook Farm Books, 1994.

Tolan, Stephanie S. *A Time to Fly Free*. New York: C. Scribner's Sons, 1983.

Information about the BOOKS MENTIONED

Bruchac, Joseph. *Keepers of the Earth*. Golden, Colo.: Fulcrum Publishing, 1991.

Feagles, Anita MacRae. *27 Cats Next Door*. New York: Young Scott Books, 1965.

Howe, Deborah and James. *Bunnicula*. New York: Atheneum, 1979.